CHAIR YOGA FOR WEIGHT LOSS

Discover Strength, Mobility and Flexibility. Look and Feel Great in Just 10 Minutes Daily. Exercise Book for Seniors over 60

Aria Sage

Paperback ISBN: 979-8-9926575-2-4

Hardback ISBN: 979-8-9926575-3-1

YOUR EXCLUSIVE ACCESS

Thanks a million for being here. Your support means so much to me!

The best way to keep in touch with me is by signing up for my newsletter – https://theawesomereaders.com/

Or scan the QR Code below

See you soon,

Aria Sage

TABLE OF CONTENTS

INTRODUCTION

The thought of growing old is scary but it is also inevitable. On one hand, it is a privilege to grow old especially if you have truly lived your life. But on the other hand, aging comes with its own set of challenges. Stiff joints, reduced mobility, slower metabolism, and weight gain that feels impossible to manage are just some of the many challenges you will have to overcome if you want to stay in great shape as you age. You may have the desire to stay active but quickly find that traditional exercise routines are too intense or physically demanding. This is where chair yoga comes in. Chair yoga is a gentle yet effective practice that allows you to build strength, improve flexibility and even lose weight. And you can enjoy all these benefits while seated or using a chair for support.

This book ***Chair Yoga for Weight Loss:*** *Discover Strength, Mobility and Flexibility, Look and Feel Great in Just 10 Minutes Daily, Exercise Book for Seniors over 60* is designed to guide you through a simple but effective approach to weight loss and overall well-being using chair yoga. Here, you will discover how regular movements can help boost your metabolism, improve circulation in your body and activate muscles that support healthy weight management. But beyond simply losing that extra weight, chair yoga is about helping you to gain strength, improve your balance, and enhance flexibility. With all of this, you are able to move through life with greater ease. If you push yourself deeper (not harder), practicing chair yoga will provide the space and opportunity that supports mental clarity, emotional balance and helps you to develop a positive outlook about life in general. All of this puts you in tip top shape both physically and mentally.

When you use this book, you will discover;

- **Simple, easy-to-follow chair yoga routines** that cater to all levels of mobility

- **Breathing techniques** to reduce stress and enhance relaxation

- **Mindfulness and meditation practices** to support emotional and mental well-being

- **Tips for staying motivated** and making yoga a sustainable part of your daily life

- **Guidance on adapting movements** to suit your body's unique needs

If this sounds like something you want to aim for, you have already taken the first crucial step on your journey. Inside the pages of this book you will find everything you need to succeed. From step-by-step chair yoga exercises to tips on breathing, posture, and modifications for different ability levels. To make chair yoga a sustainable part of your daily routine, you will also learn how to set goals that are aligned with your personal objectives and track the progress you make every step of the way. Additionally, you will explore how mindful movement, proper hydration, and simple lifestyle changes can enhance your results. The best part of all of this is that you don't need any fancy equipment or prior yoga experience. You will be working with things that you most certainly have. A sturdy chair, a willingness to move, and a commitment to your well-being.

If at any point you have ever felt discouraged by traditional fitness programs or worried that exercise is no longer for you, think of this book as your fresh start. Something to keep in mind as you make your next move is this fact: the key to success is not perfection but consistency. You will find that in this book, a lot of emphasis is placed on taking small, manageable steps each day. With a little patience and practice, you will start noticing real changes in how you feel, the way you move, and even how you see yourself as you begin practicing chair yoga. So, find a comfortable seat, take a deep breath and get ready to embark on a journey to better health, renewed energy, and a stronger, more vibrant you!

CHAPTER ONE
UNDERSTANDING CHAIR YOGA

Staying active in your senior years can be a bit of a struggle especially with traditional exercise. This is because as you age, your body faces challenges attributed to joint pain, limited mobility and balance concerns among other things. Chair yoga offers you a gentle yet powerful solution as it allows you to stretch, strengthen and improve flexibility without strain or risk of injury. In this chapter, we are exploring what chair yoga is, how it benefits your body (and mind) including supporting weight loss and how to practice it safely. At the end of this chapter, you will have a clear understanding of how to use this book as a guide to chair yoga.

CHAIR YOGA PRACTICE

Chair yoga is a gentle and more accessible form of yoga that allows you to enjoy its benefits which includes improvement in the areas of movement, flexibility and strength without the need to get on the mat to perform complex poses. In place of relying completely on your body, a sturdy chair is used to serve as your support hence the name. This form of yoga makes it possible for you to stretch your limbs, strengthen your muscles and balance your body in a safe and controlled way. And it doesn't matter if you are dealing with joint pain, recovering from an injury or simply looking for a comfortable way to stay active, chair yoga is perfect as it adapts to your needs. You can still get all the powerful benefits without having to face the intimidation of traditional yoga. A typical chair yoga session includes;

- Gentle stretching to loosen muscles and improve flexibility.

- Breath-focused movements to promote relaxation and focus.

- Seated postures that help with posture, strength, and circulation.

- Guided relaxation and mindfulness to reduce stress and improve mental clarity.

The movements in chair yoga are designed to improve circulation, reduce stiffness, and build strength over time. And because the chair used in this practice provides stability, you are able to ease into each movement without fear of losing balance. One of the best things about chair yoga is that it is compatible with all fitness levels. Even if you don't have any prior yoga experience, lack a high level of flexibility or maybe you don't even have a large space to practice, you can make it work. The fact that you can modify every pose to match your ability whether that means making a movement smaller, using extra support, or simply focusing on your breath and posture creates the ideal setup you need to achieve your goal of staying active and physically fit.

However, beyond physical fitness, chair yoga also nurtures your mental and emotional well-being. It encourages things like mindfulness, helps you to reduce stress, and puts you in a better position to feel more in tune with your body. A lot of people find that practicing chair yoga (even for a few minutes a day) improves their mood, boosts their energy, and creates a sense of calm. So whatever your objectives are, whether you want to lose weight, improve mobility, or simply feel better in your body, with chair yoga you are able to achieve your goals, one breath and one movement at a time.

HOLISTIC BENEFITS

Contrary to what people think, chair yoga is more than just a series of stretches. It is a focused holistic practice that benefits your entire well-being. Physically, it provides you with everything needed to support healthy weight loss along with your other physical goals. The gentle movements you practice will engage your muscles. This will help to speed up your metabolism and burn calories, even if you are in a seated position. Over time, this improves mobility. Everyday activities like standing, walking, picking up grandchildren or simply reaching up for things become easier and more comfortable. Unlike most high-impact exercises, chair yoga puts minimal stress on the joints, making it a safe and effective way for you to stay active at any age. It also means that recovery time for your muscles and joints does not interfere with your regular activities unlike traditional exercises.

Beyond the physical benefits, chair yoga sharpens your mind and balances emotions. During chair yoga sessions, you will engage in mindful movement and deep breathing, both of which helps to reduce stress and anxiety. It has been documented that stress and anxiety can contribute to weight gain, unstable emotions and general unhealthy habits. When you take time to connect with your body (something that comes with chair yoga practice), you become more aware of your emotions and the choices you make as a result. Things like how you eat, how you move, and how you care for yourself becomes a priority. This kind of mental clarity makes it easier to stay committed to your health goals. Plus, the sense of accomplishment you get from regular practice boosts confidence and reinforces a positive relationship with your body.

If you are looking for spiritual benefits, chair yoga offers a sense of peace and connection. It encourages you to slow down, breathe deeply, and be present in the moment. When facing life's challenges, this can be a powerful tool in managing them by bringing a sense of calm and gratitude to your daily routine. So whatever your objectives are, whether you want to practice meditation, indulge in more self-care, or simply find a way to feel more centered, chair yoga nurtures both your body and soul. By incorporating it into your life, you will not just be working toward weight loss. You will be engaging in a sustainable practice that supports your entire well-being.

HOW TO USE THIS BOOK

The entire setup of this book is designed to be your personal guide to chair yoga. Everything you need to get started is broken down to make it easy to integrate movement into your daily routine without going overboard. The best part is that you don't need to commit hours of your day. Even just 10 minutes can make a difference in how you feel. You can start your morning with a gentle stretch, take a midday movement break, or choose to unwind before bed. These short sessions will help improve flexibility, strength, and even aid in weight loss over time. The key as always is consistency. You can follow along with the exercises as they are laid out in the book or mix and match based on your needs for the day.

To get the most out of this book, it is highly recommended that you treat it as both a reference and a companion on your journey to better health. As you grow more comfortable, you should explore more strength-building and metabolism-boosting exercises designed to enhance weight loss. If you are completely new to chair yoga, start with the basics like breath awareness, simple stretches, and gentle movements. Don't skip any section because each chapter builds on the last. The contents of each section guides you step by step through mindset, movement, and lifestyle habits that support your well-being. Don't feel like you have to get to the end immediately. There is no rush, no pressure. Just allow progress to happen at your own pace and don't forget to listen to your body along the way.

Finally, the best way to integrate chair yoga into your life is to make it an enjoyable part of your daily routine. Choose a comfortable space that empowers you, wear clothing that allows you to move freely, and create a chair yoga routine that fits into your schedule. We will talk about this more in subsequent chapters. To fit this seamlessly into your regular daily routine, you can practice while watching TV, listening to music, or even in the company of friends. The idea is to get comfortable with the idea that movement feels good instead of approaching it like another chore on your to-do list. The more you make chair yoga a natural part of your day, the more you will experience its benefits. This won't be just in weight loss, but in your energy levels, confidence boost and overall well-being.

PRECAUTIONS AND SAFETY

Obviously, chair yoga is a gentle practice. However, like any form of movement, it's important to prioritize safety to prevent discomfort or any potential injury. The first step in that process is choosing the right chair. You want one that is sturdy and stable. Choose one that doesn't have wheels unless it can be locked. A chair with a straight back and no armrests is preferable because it allows for a full range of motion with minimal risk of injury. Next, always ensure that you place your chair on a non-slip surface to prevent sliding, and if necessary, keep it near a wall for extra support. Also, before you begin each session, take a moment to check your posture. Sit tall, with both feet flat on the floor and your back comfortably aligned.

Another very important rule that you must strictly adhere to for your safety is listening to your body. Chair yoga might be gentler and easier but at a certain age, you are more prone to injuries even if the activities are mild. Your body can give you cues that indicate you might be pushing yourself too hard. You must pay attention to these cues. Chair yoga movements should feel gentle and comfortable, never forced. If you experience sharp pain, dizziness, or discomfort, stop immediately and take a break. Take things a step further by modifying poses as needed. Smaller movements are just as effective as bigger ones. If you have any medical conditions, such as arthritis, osteoporosis, or high blood pressure, consult with your doctor or members of your healthcare team before starting. They can provide guidance on which movements are best for your needs and advise you on any precautions you should take. Always bear in mind that chair yoga is about healing and strengthening the body, not pushing it to its limits.

Breath awareness is another key aspect of safety as you practice. Taking deep, steady breaths helps prevent tension and allows your body to move more freely. Holding your breath, doing your breathing wrongly or moving too quickly can cause strain. So focus on slow, controlled movements. To support your breathing and movements, hydration is also essential. Drink water before and after your practice to stay refreshed. Finally, don't just rush through the exercises. Take your time. Enjoy the process. Your chair yoga sessions are not going to look or feel like those impressive workout routines but trust that even small movements can create big improvements in your strength, flexibility, and overall well-being. By taking these precautions, you can practice chair yoga with confidence knowing that you are caring for your body in the best possible way.

CHAPTER TWO
GETTING STARTED: MINDSET AND PREPARATION

When starting any new habit, especially one that involves movement, the actual journey begins with the right mindset and preparation. If you want to successfully integrate chair yoga into the way you live, you have to view it as more than just exercise. You must look at it as a lifestyle that supports your body, mind, and overall well-being and then embrace it completely. In this chapter, we will explore how to assess your health, set clear and achievable goals, and create a comfortable space for your practice. You will also learn about simple tools that can enhance your chair yoga experience. By taking the time to prepare both mentally and physically, you make it easier to stay consistent and enjoy the journey ahead.

ASSESSING YOUR HEALTH

Before you begin your chair yoga journey, it's important to take a moment to assess your health in order to understand what your body needs. Everyone's body is different. Three words you will hear frequently about this journey are mobility, strength, flexibility and that is because all of them play a role in how you move. Your past injuries should also be factored in when you conduct that self-assessment. Next on that checklist when assessing your health is your current activity level. Are you someone who already moves daily? How long has it been since you last exercised? As you ponder on those questions, consider any areas of stiffness, discomfort or chronic pain you might have on your body. Carry out a simple self-check to observe how easily you can stand up from a chair, lift your arms or turn your head. This can give you insight into which areas need extra attention.

If you have any medical conditions such as arthritis, osteoporosis or high blood pressure, it's a good idea to check with your doctor before starting chair yoga. They can help you understand any precautions to take and suggest movements that will benefit you most. Chair yoga is designed to be gentle, but as mentioned earlier, even small movements can have a big impact so you have to apply caution. Start with slow, controlled motions. And most importantly, pay attention to how you feel. If anything causes pain or discomfort, you either modify the movement or take a break. The goal is to move in a way that supports healing and strength.

Once you understand your body's needs, you can handle your chair yoga sessions with confidence. One of the many ways to track any progress you make along the way is by keeping a simple journal. Try to write down how you feel before and after each session. Make notes on any improvements in your mobility, energy levels and your general well-being. Over time, you will start to notice positive changes, even if they are only small at first. The more aware you are of your body's transformation, the more motivated you will be to create a practice that works for you. Remember, yoga isn't about perfection. It is about progress, no matter how slow or gentle the journey may be.

SETTING INTENTIONS AND GOALS

To stay motivated and make the most of your chair yoga journey, setting intentions and clearly defined goals is essential. Unlike traditional fitness programs that tends to focus mostly on physical results, chair yoga encourages a more holistic approach. If done right, it provide improvement in your mind, muscle and body in the areas of clarity, strength and flexibility respectively. But this can only be achieved if you set your goals and intentions the right way. To do this, instead of setting unrealistic expectations (which ultimately causes you to lose interest), start by asking yourself what you truly want to achieve. Do you want to feel stronger? Move more easily? Boost your energy levels? Or perhaps your goal is simply to create a daily habit of movement. By setting clear goals and meaningful intentions, you will stay inspired and focused on the bigger picture.

When it comes to weight loss, consistency is key. This is no different if you intend to use Chair yoga to achieve your goals. But have it in mind that while chair yoga can support a healthy metabolism, the practice is not just about burning calories. The focus is getting you to build a sustainable lifestyle that makes you feel good about yourself and your body. So instead of treating each session like another mega gym moment, aim to set small, achievable goals, like practicing for 10 minutes a day or focusing on deep breathing during each session. In time, these small actions add up. You will start to see a gradual weight loss. This will eventually lead to improved balance and greater confidence in your body. On this journey, progress isn't always measured by the number you see on a scale. You have to pay attention to how you feel. Being more energized, more mobile and more in tune with your body should be the primary objective.

After setting your intentions (which are about the actions you take right now) and clearly defining your goals (which are about what you want to see in the future), you want to make sure that you are able to follow through on them. So to make your goals stick, write them down and place it somewhere visible. This would make you revisit them often. That way, you are constantly reminded to stay on top of things. Let's say maybe you want to improve your posture, reduce muscle stiffness, or simply enjoy a few moments of calm each day. Whatever it turns out to be, this will serve as a reminder that shows you why you started, prompts you to take action and celebrate every small victory along the way. Know that some days will be easier than others. However, what matters most is that you keep going. Commit to taking care of yourself, one gentle movement at a time.

CREATING YOUR SPACE

Where you practice your chair yoga sessions matters a lot. Creating a comfortable space for this can make a big difference in how enjoyable and effective it feels. However, you don't need a fancy setup to get things going. What you want is just a quiet, clutter-free area where you can move freely. Choose a sturdy chair with a flat seat (a cushion is not bad) placed on a non-slip surface to prevent shifting. Avoid anything on wheels. A space that has good lighting and fresh air can also enhance your experience by making the space feel inviting. If you don't have a whole room to dedicate to this, that is just fine. A cozy corner of your living room, a spot by a window, or even outdoors on a patio is enough for a space dedicated to helping you to create a sense of routine and focus.

The little details you put into your space can also improve your practice. Where possible, remove distractions like loud noises or unnecessary furniture that might get in the way. Keeping a water bottle nearby will keep you hydrated, and a small cushion or folded towel can provide extra support when needed. Some people enjoy playing soft background music or lighting a candle to create a calming atmosphere. This not exactly essential but it is a nice addition to make your practice space feel like a peaceful retreat. The idea is to create a place that you look forward to spending some time in each day.

Your chair yoga space should project comfort, support, and ease of access for you. All of this can be present even if you have limited space. You can even do an outdoor setup if the atmosphere and surrounding ambience is right. Always remember that the key is to set up your chair wherever you feel most relaxed and ready to move. By creating an environment that not only looks good but feels good, you will find yourself naturally becoming more consistent with your practice. In turn, this makes it easier to turn chair yoga into a habit that supports your overall health and body goals.

TOOLS AND EQUIPMENT

One of the best things about chair yoga is that it requires very little equipment. You could say that with just a sturdy, comfortable chair and a desire to move, you are good to go. Your chair doesn't have to be anything fancy. It is best to use one that is bare and with no handles. A non-slip surface under the chair can provide extra stability. You can use a rug or yoga mat for that if you are indoors. But it is also fine to work with the bare ground as long as it is not slippery. A nice cushion or folded towel can provide comfort and support, especially for your lower back during certain poses. Let your body decide what it needs in those moments. Unlike traditional yoga, there is no need for a mat, blocks, or straps unless you choose to use them for modifications.

While you don't need much to get started, there are a few optional tools that can enhance your practice. As you grow and continue to build up your strength and mobility, you might need to challenge your body a little bit more to continue to enjoy the benefits of your practice. Using a resistance band can help with strength-building exercises, while small hand weights (or even water bottles) can be used to gently engage your muscles. On the other hand, using a yoga strap or belt can assist with stretches if you have limited flexibility. Now when it comes to your choice of workout clothes, choose comfortable clothing that allows you to move freely. Avoid anything that feels too tight or restrictive. Colors don't matter as long as you feel amazing wearing it. Finally , it doesn't hurt to have water nearby to stay hydrated. This is important actually and you will find out why later on. Don't forget to set up a quiet timer to keep track of your practice time.

As for what you don't need, anything complicated or expensive falls into that category. Chair yoga is designed to be accessible, meaning you can do it anywhere with what you already have. So don't feel pressured to buy special gear. Your body and your chair are the most important tools. This practice is about movement and mindfulness, not fancy equipment. The simpler your setup, the easier it is to stay consistent. The focus should be on how you feel, not what you own. Now that you have everything you need, the next step is to explore the fundamentals of chair yoga. In the next chapter, we'll dive into the basic movements, breathing techniques, and core principles that will form the foundation of your practice. Whether you are completely new to yoga or just adjusting to a seated practice, these fundamentals will help you feel confident and ready to move forward.

CHAPTER THREE
THE FUNDAMENTALS OF CHAIR YOGA

Before getting into chair yoga exercises, it's important to understand the fundamentals that will guide your practice. In this chapter, you will be introduced to important aspects of chair yoga such as gentle warm-ups, breath awareness, as well as the core principles of movement. You will also learn how to modify poses to suit your comfort level. This way, you can ensure that your practice is both safe and effective. With a strong foundation in your breath and movement practices, you can maximize each session to experience the benefits of chair yoga while gaining confidence with each step you take.

WARM-UP AND GENTLE MOVEMENTS

Warming up is an essential part of any movement practice and chair yoga is no exception. A proper warm-up prepares your muscles, joints, and circulatory system for movement. This is particularly helpful in reducing the risk of stiffness or strain. Since chair yoga is gentle, your warm-up doesn't need to be intense. It simply helps wake up the body and ease you into those gentle motions. Warm up activities like rolling your shoulders, turning your head side to side, or stretching your arms overhead can help loosen tight muscles without requiring anything too strenuous or rigorous. Even deep breathing combined with small movements can activate your body in a way that signals it is time to move.

Beyond just preparation, warm-ups play a role in boosting your metabolism. Targeted gentle seated exercises are designed to increase blood flow. This helps in delivering oxygen and nutrients to your muscles. Which in turn assists your body to burn calories more efficiently. A few minutes of gentle movement can also awaken your nervous system, improving coordination and reaction time. So whether it is tapping your feet, circling your wrists and ankles, or gently twisting your spine, carrying out these small motions will help you transition from stillness to movement smoothly.

Another great thing about warm-ups is that they also help you connect with your body. By starting your session slowly, you become more aware of how you feel on any given day. This lets you know whether you need to go easy on a certain area or if you have more energy to give. Let's not forget that chair yoga isn't about rushing through poses but about tuning in and moving with intention. A good warm-up sets the stage for a rewarding session, helping you feel more comfortable, energized, and ready to flow into deeper movements with confidence.

WARM-UP ROUTINE

You can do these altogether in one session if you have the time. Or pick a few of them if you don't. But you have to perform this entire routine along with your chair yoga session at least once a week. Remember to move slowly and breathe deeply as you perform them. These are very simple activities however, you have to make it a habit to listen to your body every step of the way.

Breathing Warm-Up

Sit tall in your chair with feet flat on the floor. Relax.

Place your hands on your belly and take a slow, deep breath in through your nose. Feel your belly expand as you do this.

Now exhale gently through your mouth. Let your shoulders relax.

Repeat 3–5 times to calm the mind and center yourself.

Neck Stretches

While holding your current sitting position, slowly tilt your head to the right. Bring your ear toward your shoulder. Hold for a breath, then switch sides.

Now gently turn your head to look over your right shoulder, then to your left.

Repeat each movement 2–3 times to release any tension in the neck.

Shoulder Rolls

Lift your shoulders up toward your ears. Hold for a breath and then slowly roll them back and down.

Repeat 5 times, then reverse the direction, rolling forward 5 times.

This helps improve posture and loosen up tight shoulders.

Seated Side Stretch

Place your right hand on the chair seat for support. Raise your left arm overhead and gently lean to the right.

Hold for a breath, then switch sides.

Repeat twice on each side to open up the spine and ribcage.

Seated Marching

Sit tall and gently lift one foot a few inches off the ground. Hold for a few seconds and then lower it back down.

Alternate legs in a slow, marching motion.

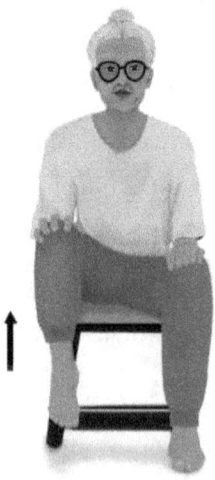

Continue for about 30 seconds to warm up the hips and legs.

Gentle Spine Twist

Place your right hand on the left knee and gently twist your torso to the left, looking over your shoulder as you do so.

Hold for a breath, then switch sides.

Repeat twice on each side to loosen the spine and improve mobility.

Once you've completed this warm-up, your body will be ready for a full chair yoga session!

BREATH AWARENESS

Breathing is something we do naturally and as a result we often take it for granted. What you probably don't realize is that when breathing is done with awareness, it becomes a powerful tool for both relaxation and weight loss. Proper breathing helps activate your body's natural energy systems and improves oxygen flow and circulation. This increased oxygen intake also fuels your metabolism, helping your body convert stored energy into movement more efficiently. Deep, intentional breaths engages your diaphragm, strengthens your core muscles and supports a better posture. Simply put, the way you breathe can influence how energized or sluggish you feel during exercise.

Apart from these physical benefits, intentional breathing techniques can also play a key role in relaxation. Many of us breathe in short, shallow bursts. This becomes amplified when we are under stress. That kind of breathing can make your body feel tense and tired. Chair yoga encourages slower, deeper breaths which are proven to calm the nervous system and reduce cortisol levels, the stress hormone that several studies have linked to weight gain. By introducing awareness to how you breath, you are able to focus on long, steady inhales and exhales. This way, you create a sense of ease in your body, making movements feel more fluid and natural. This type of breathing also helps regulate heart rate and blood pressure, promoting overall well-being.

The beauty of breath awareness is that it extends beyond your yoga sessions. You could be sitting, walking or even winding down for bed and engage in mindful breathing to center yourself and establish control over your emotions and state of mind. The more you practice these breathing techniques, the easier it becomes for you to use your breath as a tool for both movement and relaxation. In chair yoga, every pose is punctuated by steady breathing. This allows you to move with greater focus and ease. On days when physical activities are just not possible for you, a good breath session can get blood pumping in your body giving you some of the benefits of movement while allowing you to rest and recover. Here are a few breath techniques to get you started.

SIMPLE CHAIR YOGA BREATHING ROUTINE

This breathing routine helps you relax, improve oxygen flow, and enhance focus during your chair yoga practice. You can do them before, during, or after a session.

Centering Breath

Sit tall in your chair with feet flat on the ground and hands resting on your lap.

Close your eyes or soften your gaze.

Take a slow, deep breath in through your nose and then count to four. Feeling your belly expand during that time

Now exhale gently through your mouth and count to four as you do so. Feel whatever tension you experience melt away.

Repeat 3–5 times to calm the mind (and prepare for movement if you are doing this before a session).

Belly Breathing

Place one hand on your belly and the other on your chest.

Inhale deeply through your nose. Feel your belly rise while keeping your chest still.

Exhale slowly through your mouth, allowing your belly to fall.

Continue for 5–6 breaths to encourage deep, full breaths and reduce stress.

Box Breathing

Inhale through your nose for a count of four.

Hold your breath for a count of four.

Exhale slowly for a count of four.

Hold again for a count of four before repeating.

Do this 4–5 times to improve focus and bring a sense of balance.

Energizing Breath

Sit up straight and tall in your chair. Inhale deeply through your nose.

Exhale with a gentle sigh through your mouth, relaxing your shoulders.

Repeat the inhale and exhale process but this time, make it faster.

Take 3 slow breaths, then increase the pace slightly to feel more energized.

This helps boost oxygen flow and wake up the body.

Closing Breath

Return to slow, natural breathing.

With each inhale, think of filling yourself with calm and strength.

With each exhale, release any lingering tension or worry.

Repeat for 5 breaths, ending with a peaceful smile.

Use these breath techniques as a standalone relaxation practice or weave them individually or all together into your chair yoga sessions to maximize the benefits.

CORE PRINCIPLES

The core principles of chair yoga are alignment, balance, and engagement. These principles or pillars are what make each movement effective and safe. With proper alignment, you are able to ensure that your body is positioned correctly this will reduce strain on your joints and muscles. This may sound complicated but in chair yoga, it simply means sitting with your feet flat on the floor, spine tall, and shoulders relaxed. Small adjustments, like keeping your knees in line with your hips or avoiding slouching when you practice, can make a big difference in how comfortable and beneficial each movement feels. Good alignment not only prevents discomfort but also helps you move with greater ease and confidence.

Balance in chair yoga is about providing support for both your safety and strength. As we age, maintaining balance becomes more important to prevent falls and improve coordination. Chair yoga allows you to reestablish balance gradually by practicing controlled movements while you are seated. From this position, you are engaging your core muscles (those deep stabilizers in your abdomen and lower back) and this helps to create a solid foundation for every pose. Simple exercises, like lifting one foot slightly off the ground while keeping your posture steady, can train your body to find stability without strain. With consistent practice over time, these small efforts lead to better overall control, both on and off the chair.

Finally, engagement is what brings those movements to life. It turns what we feel is just passive stretching into active, meaningful exercise. Instead of simply holding a pose, chair yoga teaches and encourages you to be mindful of how each part of your body is working. When you are engaging your core, pressing your feet firmly into the floor, or gently activating your arm and leg muscles can transform even the simplest movements into effective exercises. This kind of intentional movement not only enhances strength and flexibility but also helps you stay present in your practice. When you bring all three elements together in a single session, chair yoga becomes a powerful way to move with purpose and control.

MODIFICATIONS

One of the touted strengths of chair yoga is its ability to adapt to different fitness levels and physical needs. It is a fact that no two bodies are the same. Certain things such as joint pain, limited mobility that could otherwise preclude you from participating in any physical activity are not hindrances in chair yoga practice because modifications allow you to move safely and comfortably. The key as mentioned previously is to listen to your body and then adjust movements in a way that works for you. If a stretch feels too intense, you can ease off or reduce the range of motion. If a pose requires lifting your legs and that feels too challenging, you can keep your toes on the floor while engaging your muscles. Whatever the case, every movement can be tailored to meet you exactly where you are.

Modifications also help you build confidence in your practice. Instead of feeling pressured to match a certain level of flexibility or strength which is typical in most types of workout, chair yoga encourages you to focus on what feels good for your body through modifications. Using a cushion for extra support, keeping your movements smaller, or holding onto the sides of the chair for stability are all simple ways to make exercises more accessible. As you gain strength and mobility, you can gradually progress to deeper stretches and more challenging variations. Chair yoga is designed to grows with you so no matter what, there is always a way to adapt movements to match your abilities.

If you were always very physically active, you might struggle with introducing modifications to your routines but you have to always remember that modifying doesn't mean doing less. It simply means practicing smarter. Yoga has always been about connection, not competition. So whether you are adjusting movements for comfort or to accommodate an injury, understand that every small effort counts toward improving your well-being. The more you embrace modifications, the more enjoyable and sustainable your practice will become. Don't make it about pushing through discomfort. That just sets you up for a fall. Find a way to move that feels right for you and work with it. Every small adjustment you make in posture, breath or movement, contributes to a more effective and enjoyable experience. Perfection is not the aspiration here. Focus should be on progress and consistency. In the next chapter, we will explore how chair yoga supports physical well-being as you work towards your weight loss goals.

CHAPTER FOUR
PHYSICAL WELL-BEING THROUGH CHAIR YOGA

We know what chair yoga is as well as some of the benefits. But how does truly support your physical well-being? Undoubtedly, staying physically active becomes more challenging as we age. The challenges of dealing with stiffness, joint pain, or limited mobility makes it even tougher. Many traditional exercise routines can feel too intense or intimidating, making it easy to fall into a cycle of inactivity. But we already know that movement is essential for maintaining strength, flexibility, and overall well-being. This chapter focuses on how chair yoga can help improve your physical well-being in a way that feels safe and accessible. It brings you specific chair yoga exercises created to enhance flexibility, build strength, improve posture, and prevent injuries, all from the comfort of your chair.

FLEXIBILITY AND MOBILITY

Flexibility and mobility are key to maintaining a strong, pain-free body, especially as we age. If you stop moving regularly, your muscles tighten and your joints become stiff. This would end up making everyday tasks like bending, reaching, or even walking more difficult. Chair yoga gently encourages movement in a way that keeps your joints lubricated and your muscles lengthened. This is key in reducing stiffness and discomfort. Simple stretches, such as seated spinal twists or gentle leg extensions, help loosen tight areas and restore a greater range of motion. The more you move, the more your body adapts, making daily activities feel easier and more natural.

Beyond just feeling more limber, improved flexibility and mobility can also contribute to weight loss. When your body moves freely, your metabolism functions more efficiently. In this state, you can burn calories even during low-impact activities. Chair yoga's slow, controlled movements activate various muscle groups, which increases circulation and encourages fat loss over time. Many people wrongly believe that only high-intensity workouts lead to weight loss. In truth, consistent, mindful movement helps your body stay active without unnecessary strain. You just have to ensure that you keep moving regularly and allow your body to build momentum toward better health.

Another added benefit of increased flexibility and mobility is that it helps you regain confidence in your body's abilities. When movement feels good, you are more likely to stick with it. This creates a positive cycle of activity and wellness. Chair yoga provides a safe space to stretch, strengthen, and explore what your body can do without fear of injury or discomfort. Over time, you will find that not only do you enjoy how your body feels, but you take greater pleasure in how you experience daily life. Let's look at some flexibility and mobility exercises.

CHAIR YOGA SESSION FOR FLEXIBILITY AND MOBILITY

This is a full session meant to improve joint mobility, reduce stiffness, and enhance overall flexibility. Ensure that each movement is done slowly and mindfully while seated.

Warm-Up

Sit tall with feet flat on the floor. Take a deep breath, exhale and then begin.

Roll shoulders forward in slow circles, then reverse direction.

Repeat 5–6 times in each direction.

Drop your right ear toward your right shoulder and hold for a few breaths.

Switch sides and repeat.

Next, slowly look left and right, pausing at each side.

Return to starting position and then place your right hand on the chair seat.

Raise your left arm overhead and gently lean to the right. If that feels too easy, place your left on your left knee and the raise that knee towards your chest as you stretch.

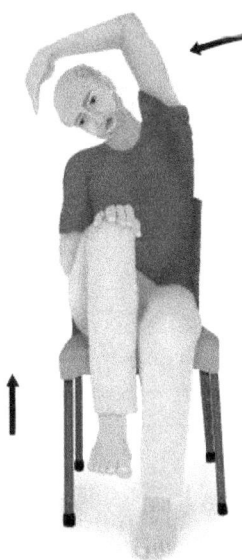

Hold for a few breaths, then switch sides.

Now place your right hand on your left knee and your left hand on the chair's backrest.

Twist gently to the left, holding for a few breaths.

Return to center and repeat on the other side. Now you are ready for the flexibility and mobility poses

Seated Cat-Cow Stretch

Place hands on your knees.

Inhale, arch your back, lift your chest, and look up (cow pose)

Exhale, round your spine, tuck your chin, and pull your belly in (Cat Pose).

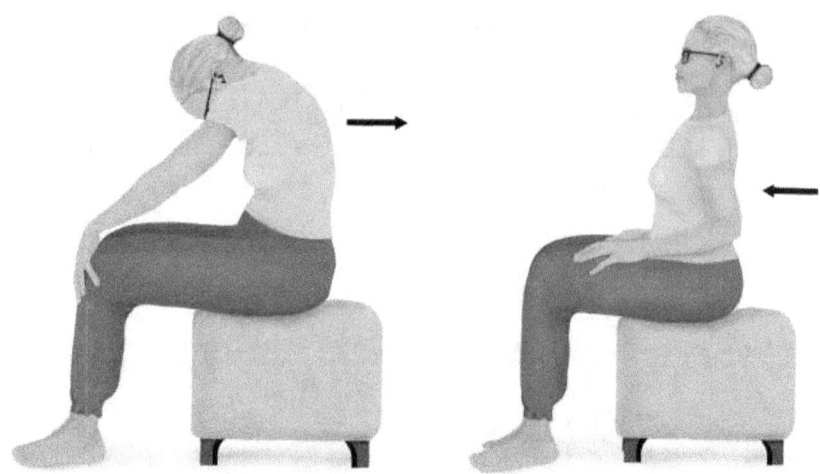

Repeat 5–6 times.

Seated Hamstring Stretch

Extend your right leg straight with the heel on the floor.

Sit tall and hinge slightly forward from your hips until you feel a stretch in your hamstring.

Hold for 5–6 breaths. Pull back your leg and then switch sides.

Repeat 3 times for each leg.

Seated Figure Four Stretch

Cross your right ankle over your left knee.

Sit up tall and gently lean forward if comfortable.

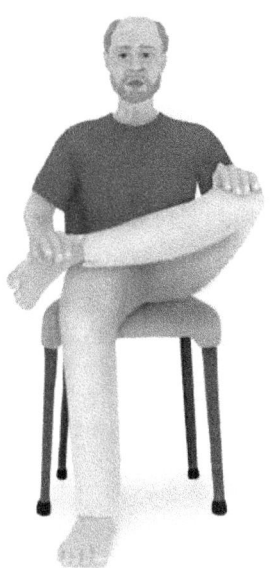

Hold for a few breaths, then switch sides.

Repeat 3 times for each leg.

Ankle Mobility Circles

Extend one leg slightly and rotate your ankle in circles.

Switch directions, then repeat with the other foot.

Do this as many times as possible

Wrist and Finger Mobility

Extend arms forward and rotate wrists in circles.

Open and close your fingers a few times.

Repeat as needed.

Seated Forward Fold

Rest hands on thighs and slowly fold forward, letting your upper body relax.

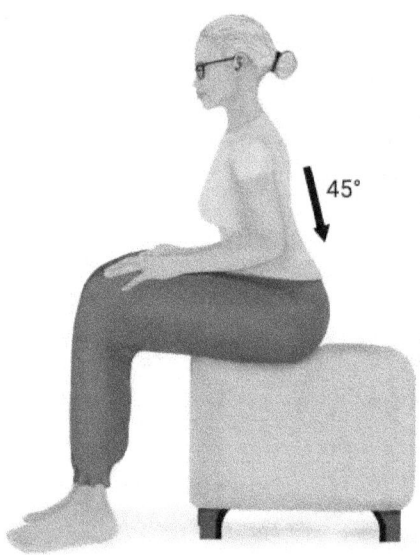

Hold for a few breaths before sitting back up.

Closing Breathwork

Sit comfortably, take a deep breath in, and exhale slowly.

Repeat for 5 breaths. Allow your body to relax and feel good about the work you have done .

This session can be done daily to maintain flexibility, prevent stiffness, and support mobility for everyday activities.

Strength and Stability

To maintain independence and prevent injuries that tend to be a frequent occurrence as one ages, strength and stability are essential. When muscles weaken, simple tasks like standing up from a chair, climbing stairs, or carrying groceries can feel more difficult. A good chair yoga session provides a gentle but effective way to build lean muscle without having to strain your body as is common in high-impact exercises. Movements like seated leg lifts, arm raises, and core-engaging postures activate different muscle groups, helping to strengthen the body from head to toe. By incorporating these small but powerful exercises into your routine, you'll develop greater stability and control over your movements.

We have talked about boosting metabolism for weight loss but your efforts to work on your body strength and stability is where it happens. Building lean muscles is generally focused on helping you to feel stronger however, an expected positive side effect of this process is that it naturally burns more calories than fat, even while at rest. So you will not be wrong in saying that by increasing muscle strength, your body becomes more efficient at using energy, which supports weight loss over time. That said, unlike traditional strength training, chair yoga prioritizes slow, intentional movements that engage muscles without the risk of strain or injury. With consistent practice on a daily, you will be able to achieve this goal.

An equally important benefit of improved strength is that it leads to better balance. This is critical in reducing the risk of falls and injuries. Many of the chair yoga exercises shared here focus on stabilizing the core, legs, and back, which are essential for maintaining good posture and coordination. As your muscles become stronger, everyday movements feel more controlled and effortless. The objective is not just to build strength but to create a body that feels steady and capable. Here's an example of a chair yoga session designed to help you build strength and work on your stability.

CHAIR YOGA SESSION FOR STRENGTH AND STABILITY

Build your muscle strength, improve balance in your movements and enhance your overall stability. Ensure that you perform each movement with deliberate control and mindful breathing.

Inhale, lift shoulders toward your ears. Exhale. Release your shoulders. Then repeat 5–6 times.

Roll shoulders forward, then backward in slow circles.

Next, adjust your sitting position so that you sit tall. Then place both of your hands on your thighs.

Inhale and let your belly full up with air. Maintain your posture. Then gently pull the belly in as you exhale. Relax.

Repeat 5–6 times to activate core muscles.

Remove your hands from your thighs and hold the sides of the chair for support. Lift one knee toward your chest. Then lower the leg slowly. Pause and alternate legs.

Do this slowly on repeat for about 30–60 seconds.

Pause to catch your breath because the next move is to enhance the seated march for better core engagement.

When you are ready, reposition yourself to sit tall. Extend your right leg straight, hold for a few seconds, then lower.

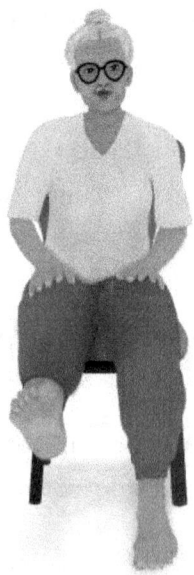

Switch to the next leg and repeat.

Do this 5 times per leg to strengthen thighs and core.

Return to start position. Place your feet hip-width apart.

Press feet into the floor and engage thighs as if you are about to stand.

Hold for 5 breaths, then relax and return to your starting position. Repeat this move 3 times.

Revert to your start position. Place your feet hip-width apart. Now lift your heels off the floor. Then slowly lower.

Repeat 10 times to strengthen calves and improve balance.

You can repeat all movements from the beginning if you have the time and feel up to it. If not, proceed to the cool down section of the session.

Sit up straight and then when you feel relaxed, lean forward slightly with arms resting on thighs.

Let your back and neck relax. Hold for a few breaths.

Return to start and repeat as many times as you need.

When you are done, sit still, take deep, slow breaths in through the nose, and then let it out through the mouth.

Reflect on your strength and progress as you do so.

POSTURAL IMPROVEMENT

A good posture is about more than just standing or sitting up straight. It does dictate how your body functions every day to an extent. When you slouch or hunch forward, it puts extra strain on your spine. This will eventually weaken your muscles and can even lead to aches and stiffness if not corrected. Consistent and proper practice of chair yoga can help you correct poor posture by strengthening the muscles that support your back, shoulders, and core. Simple movements like seated back stretches and gentle spinal twists encourage proper alignment. This makes it easier to sit tall and move with ease. As time goes, you will notice that maintaining good posture becomes second nature to you. When your posture is correct, you will feel lighter, more balanced and even more energized.

You may not be aware of this but improving your posture also has a direct impact on your breathing and digestion. When you sit up straight, your lungs have more space to expand, allowing for deeper, fuller breaths. As we have already established, engaging in deep breathing improves oxygen flow throughout the body. This goes on to increase your energy levels and reduce fatigue. As for the healthy digestion part of the equation, a better posture delivers this by preventing your abdominal organs from being compressed. Sitting tall allows food to move through your system more efficiently, reducing bloating and discomfort. It is amazing how something as simple as adjusting your posture can make a big difference in how your body processes nutrients and maintains overall wellness. But that is what this book is about; small and simple movements that deliver desired outcomes efficiently.

With the strengthening of weak muscles and a well adjusted digestive system, weight management becomes easier. You are able to move with better control and thus burn more calories throughout the day without going overboard with the exercises you perform. Additionally, good posture also encourages mindful movement. You become more aware of how you carry your body and engage your muscles. Chair yoga helps you reinforce these habits while training your body to stay aligned and strong, even when you are not exercising. Certain chair yoga practices focus primarily on fixing your posture. If this is the area you intend to work on, here are some exercises that can help you do that.

CHAIR YOGA SESSION FOR POSTURAL IMPROVEMENT

This session is specifically meant to improve alignment, strengthen postural muscles, and reduce tension in the neck, shoulders, and back.

Start with a few warm-up exercises. Sit tall, feet flat on the floor, hands resting on thighs.

Take a deep breath. Take notice of any tension in your back, shoulders, or neck.

Exhale and then gently lengthen your spine.

Inhale, lift shoulders toward ears; exhale, roll them down and back.

Repeat 5–6 times to release tension.

Tilt right ear toward right shoulder, hold for a few breaths.

Switch sides and repeat. Do this twice on each side.

Postural Correction Poses

Return to start position. Sit tall, bring arms to shoulder height, bend elbows at 90 degrees.

Bring elbows together. Squeeze shoulder blades as you do so. Hold for 5 seconds, then release.

Repeat 5–6 times to strengthen upper back muscles.

Seated Cactus Arms

Revert to starting position. Raise your arms to form a goal post position with your elbows at shoulder level.

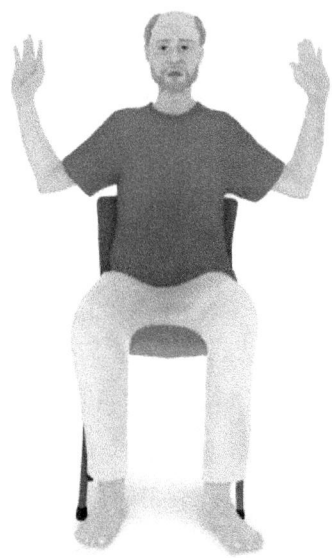

Inhale then push your arms back slightly. Hold for a few seconds. Feel your chest open.

Then exhale and relax. Repeat this 5 times.

Chin Tucks

I'm your starting position, sit tall. Relax. Take a deep breath and then exhale. Now, tuck your chin slightly back as if making a double chin.

Hold for 3–5 seconds, then release.

Repeat this 5 more times to align the neck properly.

After you are done, relax before moving on to the cool-down part of your session.

When you are ready, lean forward slightly. Rest both of your hands on your thighs.

Allow the back to lengthen and relax.

So this as many times as possible before returning to the starting position.

Sit tall, take deep breaths, and pay attention to how your posture feels.

With each inhale, lengthen the spine. And with each exhale, relax the shoulders. You return to the rest of your day when you feel ready.

INJURY PREVENTION

One of the biggest concerns when starting any exercise routine. With age, the risk of injury is higher. Strained muscles, joint pain or those famous accidental falls can slow progress and make movement feel intimidating. Chair yoga is designed to be a safe and gentle practice, but it does not completely eliminate the risk of injury. There are a few things you need to do to avoid anything that jeopardizes your safety. Simple precautions, like listening to your body, moving slowly, and never forcing a stretch, is often emphasized for keeping your practice safe and enjoyable.

You are also encouraged to work within your own limits. Don't expect to go from 0 to 100 within days. Instead focus on gradually building strength and flexibility without overexerting yourself. Because of this, learning to recognize discomfort versus pain is essential. If something doesn't feel right, adjusting or modifying a movement ensures that you can keep going without setbacks. Rather than pushing through your discomfort which is usually the underlying theme in a lot of fitness routines, here you are nudged to find a rhythm that allows for steady, long-term progress.

Another way to prevent injury is by maintaining proper form and alignment in every movement. This is true for any type of exercise. Whether you are stretching, strengthening, or simply sitting still, the way you position your body matters. Engaging your core, keeping your shoulders relaxed, and aligning your spine the right way helps to prevent unnecessary strain. The more mindful you are in your movements, the safer and more beneficial your practice becomes. By prioritizing injury prevention, you set yourself up for a practice that is both safe and rewarding. In the next chapter, we will go deeper into the mental and emotional benefits of chair yoga like how it reduces stress, improves focus, and cultivates inner peace. Just as movement strengthens the body, mindfulness strengthens the mind, creating a holistic approach to health and well-being.

CHAPTER FIVE
MENTAL AND EMOTIONAL WELL-BEING

Without doubt, life can be overwhelming. But as we age, stress, anxiety, and emotional ups and downs can feel even more challenging to manage. Many people struggle with racing thoughts, restlessness, or feelings of isolation, which can take a toll on overall well-being. Chair yoga is a powerful tool for calming the mind, lifting the spirit, and creating a sense of inner peace. This chapter explores how chair yoga can help reduce stress, improve focus, and cultivate emotional balance. Through simple breathing exercises, mindful movements, and relaxation techniques, you will learn how to quiet your thoughts, release tension, and reconnect with yourself in a way that feels refreshing and empowering.

STRESS AND WEIGHT GAIN

Before we get into those exercises, it is important to understand the connection between stress and weight gain. You see, stress isn't just a mental burden. It has a direct impact on your body, especially when it comes to weight gain. When you experience stress, your body releases a hormone called cortisol. Under normal circumstances, cortisol is meant to help you respond to challenges. However, when stress becomes chronic, your cortisol levels stay elevated, signaling your body to store fat, particularly around the belly. This is because your body thinks it needs extra energy to handle a prolonged "threat," even if that threat is just your average daily worries and anxieties. Over time, this can lead to unwanted weight gain, fatigue, and difficulty losing excess pounds. You can experience this even if you are eating well and staying active.

Chair yoga provides a gentle way to combat stress and regulate cortisol levels. The gentle movements you engage in combined with mindful breathing send signals to your nervous system that it is safe to relax. When you take slow, deep breaths and stretch your body in a calm, controlled way, you activate your body's natural "rest and digest" mode. This in turn works to lower cortisol, reduce inflammation, and shift your body from fat storage to fat burning. With consistent practice, you will notice a difference not just in how you feel emotionally but also in how your body responds to stress.

Beyond just reducing stress, when you feel calmer and more balanced, you are less likely to turn to emotional eating or unhealthy habits as a way to cope. In stressful situations, instead of feeling overwhelmed, you will have practical tools like deep breathing, gentle stretching, and mindful relaxation to handle stress in a healthier way. By taking just a few minutes each day to practice, you can break free from the cycle of stress and weight gain, allowing your body and mind to work together toward better health and well-being.

MINDFULNESS AND RELAXATION

Now that you know what the enemy is (prolonged stress), let's look at the tools you have to fight it. Mindfulness is the practice of being fully present in the moment, and when combined with chair yoga, it becomes a powerful tool for emotional well-being. A lot of us go through our days on autopilot. We react to stress, cravings, and emotions without much awareness. This can lead to emotional eating where we use food as a way to cope with boredom, sadness, or anxiety. Mindfulness in chair yoga encourages you to slow down, breathe deeply, and connect with your body. With awareness, you are able to recognize emotions as they arise without feeling overwhelmed by them. The simple act of moving with awareness can create a sense of calm and control, making it easier to respond to challenges in a healthier way.

Relaxation on the other hand is just as important as movement in chair yoga. When you engage in gentle stretches and mindful breathing, your body releases tension, and your mind naturally shifts into a more peaceful state. This relaxation response helps regulate those erratic moods and lower your cortisol levels, reducing the urge to reach for comfort foods in moments of stress. One of the many benefits of relaxation is that you no longer feel trapped in cycles of stress and emotional eating. Instead you learn how to efficiently reset and bring balance to both body and mind. The more you practice, the more you will notice how small moments of mindfulness can shift your entire day.

The combination of mindfulness and relaxation in your practice can gradually become second nature to you. You position yourself to develop a healthier relationship with the food you eat and your emotions. You will even find yourself more in tune with your body's hunger cues. Your eating schedule only happens when you are truly hungry rather than out of habit or stress. This awareness extends beyond mealtime. It influences other areas of life like improving sleep, deepening relationships with yourself and others, and basically increasing overall happiness. To summarize, you find yourself embracing a mindset that supports both your emotional balance and complete physical well-being.

BUILDING CONFIDENCE

Contrary to what people think, confidence isn't just about how you look. It is more about how you feel in your own body. As we age, it's easy to become disconnected from movement, either due to past injuries, mobility challenges, or wrong assumptions we have about old age. Chair yoga helps rebuild that connection by offering gentle, accessible movements that remind you of what your body is capable of. With each stretch, breath, and pose, you develop a greater sense of body awareness, learning to trust yourself again. This shift in perspective takes you from focusing on limitations to celebrating small victories. This lays the foundation for stronger self-esteem and a more positive outlook on health.

To support the growth of your confidence, the chair yoga practices you engage in encourages progress at your own pace. There's no competition or pressure to perform. Your primary focus is just a space to move, breathe, and grow stronger in a way that feels good for you. With time, you will notice a new sense of confidence emerging, not just in your yoga practice but in everyday life. Simple things like standing taller, moving with more ease, or feeling more in control of your body create a ripple effect that includes improved posture, soaring energy levels and a general sense of well-being. The more you practice, the more you will see that confidence is about showing up for yourself with kindness and consistency.

Along with this, chair yoga fosters a deep appreciation for your body and all that it does for you. You will learn to celebrate progress, no matter how small, instead of focusing on past struggles or worrying about what you can't do. When you feel strong, capable, and at peace with your body, it transforms the way you carry yourself in the world. You set yourself on a pathway to greater self-acceptance, resilience, and the confidence to embrace life with renewed energy and joy.

CREATING A POSITIVE MINDSET

A positive mindset is one of the most important tools for success when it comes to movement and wellness. Most people approach fitness with a critical mindset, focusing on what they need to "fix" or what they feel they are doing wrong. Chair yoga shifts this perspective by encouraging self-compassion. You learn to appreciate your body for what it can do rather than judging it for what it can't. When you approach your practice with kindness and patience, every session becomes a moment of self-care rather than another task to complete. This shift not only makes yoga more enjoyable but also keeps you motivated to show up for yourself consistently.

Gratitude is another key to staying inspired on your journey. Instead of focusing on external goals, like a number on the scale, chair yoga encourages you to celebrate how movement makes you feel. The fact that your joints feel looser, your breath comes easier, or you feel more relaxed after each session are all victories worth acknowledging and celebrating. By taking a moment to appreciate the small wins you get daily, no matter how

Chair Yoga for Weight Loss

small, you create a sense of fulfillment that goes beyond physical results. Gratitude rewires the brain to focus on progress rather than perfection, and this is a general theme throughout this book.

You have to learn to trust the process. Some days will feel easier than others, but every time you take a deep breath, stretch your body, or find a moment of stillness, you are making progress. Motivation doesn't come from forcing yourself to do something. That's a sure way to ensure that you give up on this journey somewhere along the way. True motivation comes from enjoying the process. When you create a routine that feels good, motivation follows naturally. Here's a full chair yoga session that prioritizes your mental well-being.

CHAIR YOGA SESSION FOR EMOTIONAL WELL-BEING

This gentle session helps you to cultivate calmness, reduce stress, and build a sense of confidence and positivity. The movements are simple, slow, and paired with deep breathing to promote your emotional well-being.

Grounding and Mindfulness

We will start with centering breaths.

Sit tall with your feet flat on the floor and your hands resting on your thighs.

Inhale deeply through the nose for four counts, hold for two, then exhale slowly for six counts.

Repeat 5–6 times, allowing your mind to settle as you do so.

Now place one hand on your heart and the other on your belly.

Close your eyes and think of one thing you are grateful for today. Don't overthink it. Find that little bit of blessing and connect with it.

Breathe into that feeling for a few moments.

Next, slowly tilt your head from side to side. Hold the position for a few breaths as you do so.

Shrug shoulders up to the ears, then release with an exhale.

Repeat 5 times to let go of tension. Now that you feel relaxed, we will move to confidence boosting movements.

Seated Mountain Pose

Sit tall, keep your feet grounded and your hands on your thighs.

Imagine a string lifting the crown of your head toward the sky.

Breathe deeply, feeling strong and steady. Stay with that feeling as you move to the next pose.

Open-Heart Pose

Place your hands behind your head. Keep your elbows wide.

Now take a deep breath. As you do so, lift the chest and open the heart.

Hold for a moment and then exhale, gently as you return to neutral.

Repeat 5–6 times.

Power Pose

In your seated position, place your hands on hips. Lift your chin slightly, and take deep breaths.

Hold this pose for a few moments. Enjoy the feeling of being empowered and in control.

Visualize yourself standing tall in daily life.

Seated Sun Salutation

Next, inhale. Raise your arms up overhead, stretching tall as you do so.

Then exhale as you lower arms. Imagine yourself releasing stress with each exhale.

Repeat this 5–6 times. Ensure that you sync breath with movement.

Now we will move to movements that promote relaxation and compliment this with positive affirmations

Seated Forward Fold

Rest your arms on your thighs and let your head drop forward.

Hold this position as you take slow breaths, letting go of any lingering stress.

Closing Visualization

Return to your starting position. Sit tall and close your eyes. Take those deep, gentle breaths. Now picture yourself feeling light, strong, and happy.

Silently repeat these words;

I am calm.

I am confident.

I am at peace.

Take three deep breaths. Smile gently on each exhale. Carry this positive energy with you into the rest of your day.

Now that we have explored the mental and emotional benefits of chair yoga, it's time to get deeper into how movement affects metabolism and weight loss. In the next chapter, we'll explore how chair yoga can help you burn calories, improve digestion, and activate fat loss. You will also learn how mindful movement supports a healthy metabolism and discover simple practices to help your body become more efficient at using energy.

CHAPTER SIX
METABOLISM AND WEIGHT LOSS WITH CHAIR YOGA

As we grow older losing weight and maintaining a healthy metabolism can feel like an uphill battle. Many seniors struggle with slower digestion, reduced muscle mass, and a body that doesn't burn calories as efficiently as it once did. The good news is that movement doesn't have to be strenuous to be effective. In this chapter, we will explore how chair yoga can support weight loss by gently boosting metabolism, improving digestion, and increasing muscle tone. And all can be done while being easy on the joints. By understanding how your body processes energy and learning some simple, low-impact movements that enhance fat burning, you will discover that sustainable weight loss is not only possible but also enjoyable.

UNDERSTANDING METABOLISM

We have heard the word metabolism being used in context with weight loss but what exactly is it? Metabolism is the process by which your body converts food into energy and as you probably already know, it plays a key role in weight management. Problems like muscle loss, hormonal changes, and decreased physical activity which happen as we age forces our metabolism to naturally slow down. This means your body will burn fewer calories at rest, making it easier to gain weight and harder to lose it. However, the good news is that movement even gentle, consistent exercise like the ones you are about to learn can help you to reignite your metabolism.

One of the biggest myths about weight loss is that only high-intensity workouts can boost metabolism. Undoubtedly, intense exercise burns calories fast. But it is not the only way to achieve results. Chair yoga stimulates the body in a different but equally effective way. Slow, intentional movements combined with deep breathing help oxygenate the body, improve circulation, and activate muscles (we talked about this) and all of this work to support a healthy metabolism. Even small movements, like lifting your arms or engaging your core while seated, encourage your body to work harder and burn more energy. Over time, these consistent efforts can lead to noticeable changes in strength, endurance, and overall fat loss.

We also mentioned that beyond burning calories, chair yoga also improves digestion and reduces stress. These are two factors we already know directly impacts metabolism. Gentle yoga helps regulate cortisol levels, keeping your body in a balanced state where it can burn energy efficiently. By combining movement with mindful breathing, chair yoga creates an environment where the body can function at its best, making weight loss more natural and sustainable at any age.

BURNING CALORIES WITH SEATED MOVEMENTS

You are probably one of those people who believe that to burn calories effectively, you need to engage in high-impact activities like running or weightlifting. That is one way to do it. You are reading this book to figure out how gentle seated movements can help the body burn fat and increase energy use. The chair yoga movements you will learn shortly encourages slow, controlled motions that activate different muscle groups. This act alone requires energy to perform. Whether it's a seated twist, a gentle leg lift, or an overhead stretch, these movements stimulate circulation, get your heart rate up, and encourage your body to burn calories.

One of the advantages you will enjoy is a renewed ability to engage multiple muscle groups at once without exerting yourself too much. When you move your arms, legs, and core together in a coordinated flow, your body works harder to maintain balance and stability. This means more calories are burned in a shorter amount of time. Additionally, chair yoga activities that engages your core while seated such as pulling your belly button toward your spine during a pose activates deep abdominal muscles.

This helps to tone and strengthen your midsection while improving posture and stability.

It keeps the body in motion without excessive stress on the joints. Unlike traditional workouts that can sometimes lead to injury or exhaustion, seated movements allow you to exercise safely while still reaping the benefits of calorie burn. Over time, these small, intentional movements add up, leading to increased energy levels, better muscle tone, and gradual fat loss. With proper planning, you can do these exercises anywhere, making it easy to stay active and keep your metabolism running efficiently throughout the day.

ACTIVATING CORE MUSCLES

Your core is the powerhouse of your body. It plays an essential role in balance, posture, and overall strength. But beyond helping you sit up straight and move with ease, strong core muscles also contribute to a faster metabolism, something that you are trying to achieve here. According to research, muscle tissue burns more calories than fat, even when it is at rest. When you engage your core through chair yoga, you activate those deep abdominal muscles that help tone your midsection and improve your body's ability to burn energy efficiently.

Strengthening your core also enhances stability and reduces the risk of falls and injuries. Many seniors struggle with balance as they age. Chair yoga provides a supportive way to build core strength without the fear of falling. The seemingly simple exercises encourage your abdominal muscles to engage and trains them to provide better support for your spine and lower back. Again, you get maximum benefits from minimum efforts.

With core activation comes improved digestion. A strong core supports better posture, which keeps the digestive organs in proper alignment and allows them to function more effectively. Poor posture can lead to sluggish digestion, bloating, and discomfort. This is known to slow down metabolism. By practicing chair yoga and maintaining core engagement throughout your movements, you are not only building strength but also creating a healthier internal environment for weight loss and overall well-being.

IMPROVING CIRCULATION AND DIGESTION

Good circulation and healthy digestion are important for effective weight loss, yet they are often overlooked in traditional fitness routines. Poor circulation can slow down metabolism, making it harder for the body to burn fat efficiently. Chair yoga helps combat this by focusing on gentle movements that stimulates blood flow. This ensures that oxygen and essential nutrients gets to every part of the body. This increased circulation not only boosts your energy levels but also helps your body to process food more effectively thus preventing bloating and sluggish digestion.

When your digestive system isn't functioning properly, food isn't broken down as efficiently. This will eventually lead to issues like gas, bloating, and weight gain. Certain seated movements even encourage peristalsis which is the wave-like contractions of the intestines that move food through the digestive tract. By incorporating chair yoga into your routine, you are not just moving your body. You will also giving your digestive system the support it needs to function at its best.

Finally , a point that must be addressed is detoxification. Your body naturally eliminates waste and toxins through the liver, kidneys, and lymphatic system. However, when your circulation and digestion systems are sluggish, this process can slow down. Chair yoga supports detoxification by stimulating these systems, helping the body flush out toxins more efficiently. When you combine these gentle movements with proper hydration and mindful eating, you create an internal environment that promotes fat loss, improved energy, and overall well-being. With all of this knowledge, let us a look at a chair yoga that addresses of this.

CHAIR YOGA SESSION FOR CORE ACTIVATION

This session focuses on engaging your core to stimulate digestion, boost metabolism, and promote fat loss. The movements are gentle but effective.

Warm-Up

We will start with a quick warmup.

Sit tall with your feet flat on the floor and your hands resting on your belly.

Inhale deeply through your nose. With your hand on your belly, feel it rise and expand.

Now exhale slowly through your mouth. Draw the belly in toward your spine as the air leaves your body.

Repeat 5–6 times to wake up the core and activate digestion.

Next, we will do the seated cow to cat pose. Place your hands on your knees. Inhale as you lift your chest and arch your back.

Hold for a few seconds then exhale pulling your belly inward as you round your spin.

Repeat 5–6 times to stimulate the abdominal organs.

Now we will move to core strengthening movements.

Seated Knee Lifts

Sit tall, hold the chair's sides for support.

Take a deep and then on your exhale, lift your right knee toward your chest.

On your next inhale, lower it down slowly.

Alternate legs and repeat. Do this a total of 10 times in each side.

Seated Bicycle Twists

Place both hands behind your head.

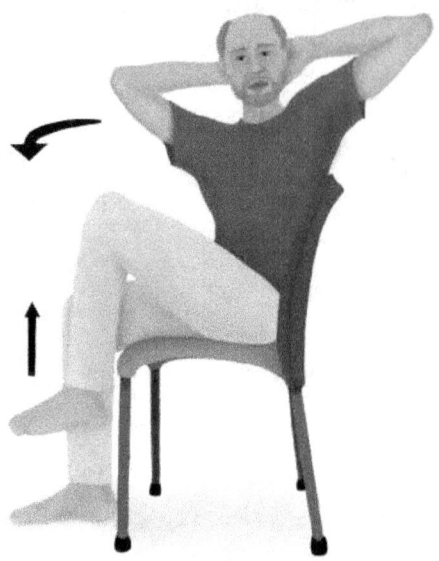

Lift your right knee and twist your left elbow toward it.

Lower and switch sides. Do this like a slow-motion bicycle.

Repeat 10 times per side to strengthen obliques and aid digestion.

Seated Leg Extensions

Return to rest position. Now extend your right leg straight out. Keep your core engaged as you do so by holding your belly in.

Hold this pose for a few seconds, then lower.

Repeat this with the left leg.

Do 10 reps per side to build core strength and boost metabolism.

You should feel some muscle burn in your mid region when you are done. Let's move to practices that will help you relax and recover.

Seated Forward Fold

Assume the starting position. Let your arms dangle over your legs, allowing gravity to relax your belly.

Then take slow breaths, as you gently massage your stomach area.

Seated Spinal Twist

Place your right hand on your left knee with your left hand on the chair's back fur extra support.

Inhale as you lengthen your spine. Then exhale as you twist gently.

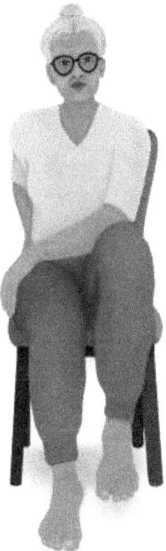

Hold for a few breaths, then switch sides.

Repeat for a few times before returning to breath works to wrap up the session.

When you are ready, sit tall, close your eyes, and inhale deeply.

Exhale slowly, imagining warmth and energy in your core.

Repeat 3 times, then smile and relax.

Now that you have a better understanding of how chair yoga influences metabolism, digestion, and circulation, you are well on your way to making lasting changes. But to see real results, consistency is key. In the next chapter, we will explore how to build a sustainable chair yoga routine that fits your lifestyle, keeps you motivated, and helps you stay on track with your weight loss and wellness goals.

CHAPTER SEVEN
BUILDING A SUSTAINABLE CHAIR YOGA ROUTINE

Starting a new routine is exciting, but sticking with it is where challenge comes in. Life gets busy, motivation fluctuates, and some days, you just don't feel like moving. You might begin an exercise plan with enthusiasm, only to struggle with consistency over time. The chair yoga routines shared here is designed to be gentle, adaptable, and easy to fit into your daily life no matter your schedule or energy levels. In this chapter, you will learn how to set realistic goals, structure your sessions, and make chair yoga a natural part of your day. Whether you have ten minutes in the morning or prefer to spread movements throughout your day, this chapter will help you find an approach that keeps you motivated and committed to your well-being.

STRUCTURING YOUR PRACTICE

A well-structured chair yoga practice doesn't have to be complicated to be effective. What you want to focus on is to create a routine that feels natural and manageable so that it easily fits into your daily life. Start by setting aside a specific time each day for your practice. This could be first thing in the morning, during a midday break or in the evening to unwind. Even just 10 minutes can make a difference. Your practice can be as simple as a warm-up, a few seated stretches, and a deep breathing exercise to finish. Remember, the goal is consistency, not perfection.

Variety is also important for keeping your routine engaging and balanced. A well-rounded session should include gentle stretches for flexibility, strength-building movements, and mindful breathing exercises. You can mix and match different exercises based on your needs each day. For example, if you wake up feeling stiff, you might focus more on mobility movements. If you want to build strength, you can incorporate seated core work or resistance exercises. Keeping your practice flexible ensures it remains enjoyable rather than feeling like some kind of rigid obligation.

To make your routine truly sustainable, connect it to an existing habit. Pair your chair yoga session with your morning cup of tea, an afternoon relaxation break, or right before bed as part of your wind-down routine. This makes it easier to stay consistent without having to carve out extra time in your schedule. It is also advisable to keep a simple journal to track your progress. Make notes on how you feel before and after each session. Over time, you will start to notice positive changes in your body and mind, reinforcing your commitment to this practice.

TIME-EFFICIENT WORKOUTS

One of the biggest misconceptions about exercise is that you need to spend hours working out to see results. Again, consistency matters more than duration. A well-planned 10-minute chair yoga session can be just as effective as a longer workout if done regularly. You need to focus on intentional movements that engage the body efficiently. By dedicating just 10 minutes a day to chair yoga, you can boost your metabolism, improve flexibility, and build strength. Thankfully, you can do all this without feeling overwhelmed or exhausted.

The secret to making short workouts effective is to include a mix of movements that target different areas of the body. A quick session might start with gentle spinal twists to warm up, followed by seated leg lifts for strength, and finish with deep breathing for relaxation. This balance ensures you are improving circulation, enhancing mobility, and activating muscles. By now you know that these are all essential for weight loss and overall well-being. By keeping your routine simple yet structured, you maximize the benefits without needing to carve out large chunks of time.

A time-efficient approach also makes it easier to stay consistent. Since 10 minutes is a manageable commitment, you are less likely to skip sessions.

Being able to stay consistent means you will see progress faster. The more regularly you move, the more your body adapts, making everyday tasks easier and keeping you motivated to continue. Over time, those short sessions will start showing up in your improved strength, better posture, increased energy, and a greater sense of well-being.

TRACKING PROGRESS

Tracking your progress is one of the best ways to stay motivated on your chair yoga journey. It's easy to overlook small improvements when you are focused on the bigger goal. But don't underestimate the impact of those small wins. You might notice that your back feels less stiff in the morning, or that you can hold a posture a little longer than before. These moments are signs that your body is growing stronger, more flexible, and more balanced. By recognizing these victories, you reinforce your commitment and keep your momentum going.

There are many ways to track your progress, and you don't need anything complicated. A simple journal where you jot down how you feel before and after each session can be a powerful tool. Noting improvements in strength, flexibility, energy levels, or even your mood can help you see just how much your practice is benefiting you. If you prefer a visual approach, try taking occasional photos or videos of yourself in different postures. This can show changes that you might have normally missed over time. You might also use a calendar to check off each day you practice, creating a sense of accomplishment as you see your consistency build.

Celebrating progress is just as important as tracking it. Reward yourself for sticking with your practice. It doesn't have to be something extravagant. Treating yourself to a relaxing tea after a session or simply taking a moment to acknowledge your dedication works. Remember that progress isn't just about weight loss or physical changes. It should be about feeling better in your body and mind. By focusing on small wins, you turn chair yoga into a joyful habit and over time, these little victories will keep you inspired to show up for yourself, day after day.

ADAPTING OVER TIME

As your body adapts to chair yoga, it's important to keep evolving your practice to maintain progress. What once felt challenging may become easier over time. This is a great sign that you are getting stronger and more flexible. To keep improving, gradually increase the intensity of your movements. This could mean holding a posture for a few extra breaths, adding light resistance with a band, or engaging your muscles more intentionally during each exercise. Small adjustments like these help ensure that your body continues to build strength, burn calories, and stay engaged in the practice.

Variety is another key to long-term success. Doing the same routine every day can eventually lead to downward path, where progress slows down and motivation dips. To prevent this, mix things up by exploring different chair yoga sequences. Some days, focus more on gentle stretching and relaxation. Other days, challenge yourself with strength-based movements. You can also experiment with breathing techniques and mindfulness exercises to deepen your mind-body connection. Keeping your practice fresh and exciting makes it easier to stay committed.

Finally, listening to your body is just as important as challenging it. There will be days when you feel strong and energized. And then you will have other days when you need to take it slow. That is perfectly normal. Chair yoga is excellent for its adaptability. You can modify movements to match your energy levels and needs. If something feels too easy, add a slight challenge. If it feels too difficult, dial it down and take a step back. This flexibility ensures that you maintain steady progress without feeling discouraged or overworked. As we wrap up this chapter, remember that a sustainable routine is one that evolves with you. In the next chapter, we will explore another essential piece of the weight loss puzzle which is nutrition and lifestyle. What you eat and how you care for yourself outside of yoga play a major role in your overall success and you need to pay attention to that.

CHAPTER EIGHT
NUTRITION AND LIFESTYLE FOR WEIGHT LOSS

Your nutrition and lifestyle play a very important role in helping you to reach weight loss goals. This is particularly important if you are looking for something to complement your chair yoga practice. As you already know by now, metabolism naturally slows down as you age, making it easier to gain weight and harder to shed those extra pounds. This chapter will provide you with practical, simple but effective strategies to nourish your body and maintain a healthy weight without restrictive diets.

HEALTHY EATING FOR SENIORS

As your body ages, its nutritional needs shift. This makes it essential for you to adopt eating habits that support energy, digestion, and overall health. We all have different individual needs but there are basic fundamentals that you can build on when finding the right nutrition for you.

PRIORITIZING NUTRIENT-DENSE FOODS

Because most people in their older years tend to eat smaller portions due to reduced appetite, it is imperative that every bite should be packed with essential nutrients. This means your focus should be on whole, unprocessed foods such as fruits, vegetables, whole grains, lean proteins and healthy fats. These foods provide vitamins, minerals, and antioxidants that help maintain muscle strength, boost immunity and keep energy levels stable.

Balancing Protein Intake

Muscle mass naturally declines with age. To fix or prevent this, protein intake is critical. It is also excellent for maintaining strength and preventing frailty. Lean sources like fish, poultry, beans, lentils, eggs, dairy and tofu are excellent choices. Protein also helps with satiety, reducing unnecessary snacking and supporting weight management.

Staying Hydrated

Many seniors become a lot less thirsty over time. This increases the risk of dehydration, which can lead to fatigue, confusion, and digestive issues. Drinking enough water, herbal teas and consuming water-rich foods like cucumbers, oranges, and soups can help maintain hydration.

Things like eating foods that are rich in fiber can also be helpful for combating digestive problems which are prevalent among the elderly. Your team of healthcare providers are in a better position to give you a detailed set of guidelines for your nutrition. This is a necessity if in addition to problems with weight, you are dealing with things like diabetes, hypertension, osteoporosis or any other illness that can impact your movement. If you pair these nutrition guidelines with your chair yoga practice, you can maintain your weight loss goals, be healthier and feel so much better.

Hydration and Its Role in Weight Loss

Proper hydration is important for your overall health. As your body ages, the sensation of thirst diminishes. This can make you prone to dehydration. When there is a lack of hydration, you will notice that your metabolism slows down and that can lead to digestive issues. You will also observe that you feel tired a lot of the time and this can impact your ability to move which is essential for weight loss. Even a simple exercise routine like chair yoga can seem like a tedious task for you.

Drinking enough water helps to regulate your body temperature, transport nutrients, and remove waste. It also helps in the breakdown of stored fat that can be converted to energy for your body. Hydration supports digestion which helps to prevent constipation and bloating. That extra glass of water can make you feel less sluggish and heavy. Another simple detail that escapes a lot of us is the fact that we sometimes mistake thirst for hunger and so when you are supposed to be drinking water, you find yourself snacking on food. However, by drinking enough water, you can better manage your appetite and reduce the likelihood of overeating.

So how can you optimize your water drinking habits to complement your chair yoga practice? First, start the day with water. This jumpstarts metabolism, flushes out toxins and rehydrates the body after sleep. Substituting a plain glass of water with one water and a little bit of lemon juice can be a refreshing and gentle way to wake up the digestive system. Next, drink a glass of water 15–30 minutes before your meals to help control portion sizes as it creates a sense of fullness. This simple habit can prevent overeating and support mindful eating. For optimum results, you should aim for at least 6–8 glasses of water daily. However, individual needs vary based on one's activity level and climate. So keep that in mind.

QUALITY SLEEP AND RECOVERY

Sleep is often overlooked in conversation around weight loss but it plays a very important role in metabolism, energy levels and overall well-being. Poor sleep can disrupt the hormones that regulate appetite and fat storage and this remains true even as you age. When sleep is insufficient, your body produces more of the hunger hormone and less of the hormone that signals fullness. This leads to increased cravings and overeating. Additionally, when you are not getting enough sleep your body produces the stress hormone that encourages it to store fat, especially, around the midsection.

The interesting thing is that not only does poor sleep lead to weight gain, it can also make weight loss more challenging. A tired body struggles to metabolize food efficiently. So what you are left with is slower digestion and increased fat retention. However, when you prioritize restful sleep, your body will function more efficiently, making it easier to maintain a healthy weight. Now if you are genuinely struggling with falling asleep, it is important to figure out how to fix that so that all the efforts you are making with your chair yoga routines are not in vain.

The fast step to a healthy sleep shadow is to create a nightly routine. It doesn't have to be something elaborate. Gentle chair yoga, deep breathing or a warm cup of herbal tea can help signal the body that it's time to rest. When you have set that night routine, the next step is to stick to your sleep schedule. Going to bed and waking up at the same time each day helps regulate your body's internal clock. To be able to maintain this avoid anything that interrupts your sleep signals. This would mean that you would have to reduce caffeine, limit your screen time before bed and avoid large meals right around your bedtime. It also doesn't hurt to create a comfortable space for you to sleep in. Choose soft beddings and soft lighting to encourage sleep.

DAILY MOVEMENT BEYOND YOGA

Chair yoga as you already know is a powerful tool for improving strength, flexibility and overall well-being. But including small daily habits can make it even more effective. There are simple lifestyle changes that can enhance mobility and promote long-term weight loss without requiring drastic efforts. By focusing on small, manageable adjustments, you can create a sustainable routine that supports your chair yoga practice and overall health. While chair yoga is an excellent form of movement, adding extra physical activity throughout the day can amplify its benefits. Simple changes like standing up every 30–60 minutes, stretching while watching TV or taking short walks around the house helps to keep your body active.

Engaging in light household chores, gardening or just dancing to a favorite song can also contribute to improved circulation and mobility. The goal is to avoid long periods of sitting still and find enjoyable ways to keep moving.

But it is not always about movement even when you are sitting or standing still, there are things you can do to complement your movement efforts. Practicing good posture outside of chair yoga sessions is one of them. It helps to maintain spinal alignment, reduce joint strain, and improve breathing. So be mindful of your posture while sitting, standing, or walking by gently pulling the shoulders back, lifting the chest, and keeping the core engaged. Over time, better posture enhances balance, prevents falls, and supports overall strength.

Stress we already know can make weight loss more difficult. But incorporating small relaxation practices such as deep breathing, meditation or gratitude journaling can help regulate emotions and keep that stress in check. That being said, one thing that keeps the ball rolling in terms of all these activities you are doing is consistency. Even small, daily habits can create lasting results when done regularly. By making small, intentional lifestyle changes alongside chair yoga, you can experience a greater sense of well-being without overwhelming effort that leads to an increased overall quality of life.

GUIDED MEDITATION FOR HEALTHY HABITS AND LASTING WELL-BEING

Begin by sitting comfortably in a sturdy chair with feet flat on the floor and hands resting gently on your lap. Close your eyes. Take a deep breath in… and slowly exhale. Let your body relax as you settle into this moment.

Take a slow, deep breath in… filling your lungs with fresh, nourishing air. And as you exhale, let go of any tension or worries. Feel your body supported by the chair beneath you, steady and strong. This moment is for you… to care for yourself… to honor your journey… and to embrace the small changes that will bring lasting well-being.

Now, bring your awareness to your body. Imagine yourself moving with ease throughout your day. See yourself standing up with strength, stretching your arms with confidence, walking with lightness. You are not bound by limitations. Each movement, no matter how small, contributes to your strength and mobility. Feel the energy of motion filling your body, keeping your joints fluid, your muscles engaged and your heart open.

As you sit here, notice your posture. Gently lift your chest, relax your shoulders, and engage your core. Feel how a small shift in posture creates a sense of lightness and balance. Take a deep breath in… and out. Imagine this awareness of posture staying with you throughout your day…whether sitting, standing, or walking. With every breath, your body aligns effortlessly, supporting your strength and well-being.

Now, shift your focus to nourishment. Picture yourself enjoying a meal…one that is wholesome and satisfying. See yourself eating slowly, savoring every bite as you listen to your body's cues. Imagine drinking a glass of water, feeling the cool hydration energize your body and refreshing your mind. Each sip fuels your well-being, keeping your metabolism active, your skin vibrant, and your digestion strong. You honor your body by giving it what it needs.

Now, imagine yourself at the end of the day, winding down for restful sleep. Your body feels relaxed, your mind at ease. You have moved with purpose, nourished yourself with care, and honored your well-being. With each breath, stress melts away. Next, say these words out loud to remind yourself of your purpose

"I am taking care of myself"

"I am creating lasting habits that support my health"

"I am worthy of this journey"

Slowly bring your awareness back to the present. Wiggle your fingers and toes gently. Take one more deep breath in… and exhale fully. When you feel ready, open your eyes. Carry this sense of mindfulness, ease, and purpose with you. Let these small, daily choices add up to a healthier, happier you.

This practice helps internalize the habits we just discussed. It reinforces mindful movement, posture, nourishment, stress management, and rest. By revisiting this meditation regularly, you can create a strong mental foundation for long-term well-being.

CHAPTER NINE
WORKING THROUGH CHALLENGES AND STAYING MOTIVATED

This chapter is all about overcoming challenges and staying motivated on your chair yoga journey. It's natural to face obstacles. On some days, you might feel too tired or struggle to find the time. Maybe you are dealing with physical limitations or simply losing enthusiasm. This chapter will help you navigate these moments with practical strategies to stay consistent, adapt to setbacks, and reignite your motivation. By the end, you'll have the tools to keep moving forward with confidence, knowing that every small effort counts toward lasting well-being.

OVERCOMING CHALLENGES

Starting a sustainable fitness journey requires more than just physical effort. It begins with the right mindset. Change at any point can feel overwhelming and setbacks are a normal part of the process. The key is to approach your journey with patience and self-compassion. Instead of seeing these challenges as barriers, view them as opportunities to learn and grow. Some days will be easier than others, but as we have emphasized so many times, what matters most is consistency, not perfection.

A strong mindset is built on realistic expectations. You may have started this wellness journey expecting instant results, but you have to understand that true transformation takes time. Chair yoga, healthy eating, and small lifestyle adjustments work together to create lasting change but those changes will not come overnight. Focus on progress and celebrate even the smallest improvements like increased flexibility, better posture or more energy. When you shift your mindset from short-term results to long-term well-being, staying committed becomes much easier.

Finally, you have to constantly remind yourself why you started. Whether it's because you wanted to feel stronger, move with ease, manage your weight or simply enjoy a better quality of life, keeping your personal "why" at the forefront of your mind will help you push through challenges. You should also remember to stay flexible in your approach. Pushing through any pain or health challenges at this point could be detrimental to you. Instead, be kind to yourself and trust that every effort you make, no matter how small, brings you closer to your goal.

DEALING WITH PHYSICAL LIMITATIONS

When you started on this fitness journey, you were already aware that you would be faced with unique challenges. But something you must have learned on your journey so far is that limitations don't mean impossibilities. You just need to make a few tweaks to adapt to your situation. With age comes wisdom along with a lot of wonderful life experiences but it also naturally brings changes to the body, such as reduced flexibility and a higher likelihood of chronic conditions. These factors shouldn't discourage you from moving and improving your well-being. Instead, they highlight the importance of a gentle, sustainable approach like chair yoga. The major tweak you have to make here is to work with your body, not against it.

Something you will encounter quite a lot here is pain and stiffness. While some discomfort is natural, exercise should never cause sharp pain or distress. Chair yoga helps you to ease into movement without putting too much strain on your joints. If you experience stiffness, start slowly with gentle stretches and deep breathing to warm up your muscles. If you are dealing with arthritis or joint pain, modify the poses and use support such as cushions or rolled-up towels to make movements more comfortable. You have to listen to your body and make adjustments as needed.

Health conditions like osteoporosis, high blood pressure or diabetes can also require modifications to your practice. For example, if you have balance concerns, you can always keep both feet on the floor rather than attempting leg lifts. If you experience dizziness or fatigue, take breaks and focus on breathing exercises to regulate your energy levels. Remember, chair yoga is adaptable. Even small, consistent movements when done correctly can lead to noticeable improvements in your body. By focusing on what you can do, you build a sustainable routine that supports your body at any stage of life.

KEEPING IT ENJOYABLE

One of the best ways to stay consistent with chair yoga is to genuinely enjoy the process. Exercise in any form shouldn't feel like a chore. It should feel like a gift to your body. Think of it as a time to reconnect with yourself and an opportunity to feel better every day. If your routine starts feeling dull or repetitive, it's a signal to mix things up. Explore different movements, try chair yoga sessions with themes like "energizing mornings" or "relaxing evenings," or simply put on some calming music while you practice. Keeping your routine fresh and engaging helps you look forward to each session rather than seeing it as just another task.

Finding joy in movement also comes from tuning into how your body feels. If you are focusing strictly on burning calories or achieving a specific look, you make the journey that much harder. Instead, shift your mindset to how each movement benefits you. Notice how stretching your spine relieves tension, how deep breathing calms your mind and how small improvements in flexibility or strength make daily activities easier. Being able to reach a little farther or sit up straighter without discomfort is cause for celebration. Recognizing these little victories keeps you motivated and reminds you why you started in the first place.

Finally, make your practice something that is personal and enjoyable. Maybe you love doing chair yoga outdoors in the fresh air. Or perhaps you enjoy following along with a guided video. You can even turn it into a social activity by inviting a friend to join you or setting up a virtual session with loved ones. The key is to make these sessions something you look forward to rather than something you "have to" do. When movement feels like a joyful part of your day rather than an obligation, it is easier for you to be consistent at it.

STAYING ACCOUNTABLE

Getting on a weight loss journey requires accountability. Staying accountable to yourself is one of the most important parts of maintaining consistency in your practice. One of the best ways to do this is by building a strong support system. Surround yourself with people who encourage and uplift you. This could be family, friends or even an online community. Let them know about your goals and share your progress with them. Having someone to check in with or practice alongside can make a big difference in staying motivated, especially on days when you feel less inspired. Even a simple phone call or message from a friend can be the push you need to stay on track.

Another powerful tool for accountability is journaling. Writing down your goals, daily experiences and progress creates room to reflect on how far you have come. Keep a simple journal where you note how you feel after each chair yoga session, any challenges you faced, and small victories along the way. On days when you feel discouraged, a quick glance through your journal can remind you of your progress and keep you motivated. You can also use it to track your energy levels, flexibility or mindset shifts. This helps to reinforce the positive impact of your practice.

Basically, staying motivated requires finding techniques that work for you. Just remember to set small, achievable goals rather than overwhelming yourself with big changes all at once. Reward yourself for consistency. This might involve treating yourself to a relaxing activity after a workout, celebrating milestones with a fun event or simply acknowledging your own dedication. Positive affirmations and visualization can also be helpful here. You use them to remind yourself why you started and picture how great you will feel as you continue. The combination of support systems, consistent journaling, and motivation techniques helps you to create a structure that keeps you accountable.

GUIDED MEDITATION FOR FOCUS AND MOTIVATION IN YOUR FITNESS JOURNEY

Begin in a comfortable seated position, either on a chair or in a quiet space where you feel at ease. Take a deep breath in... and slowly exhale. Let go of any tension in your body. Gently close your eyes or soften your gaze. This is your time. It is your moment to focus on yourself, to reconnect with your motivation, and to strengthen your commitment to your wellness journey.

Breathe in deeply, filling your lungs with fresh energy... and slowly release any doubts or distractions as you exhale. Feel your shoulders relax, your jaw soften, your hands resting gently in your lap. With each breath, allow yourself to sink deeper into a state of calm awareness.

Now, bring to mind your reason for beginning this journey. See yourself moving with ease, feeling stronger, more energized, more confident. Imagine yourself completing your chair yoga sessions with joy, feeling refreshed and accomplished. Picture the small daily efforts adding up, each movement bringing you closer to your goals.

Now, visualize your future self. See the version of you that is strong, flexible, and full of life. See yourself standing tall, feeling light and free, moving without hesitation or discomfort. Let that image fill you with confidence. You are showing up for yourself, one step at a time.

As you continue to breathe deeply, repeat these affirmations silently or aloud to yourself

"I am committed to my health and well-being"

"Every small step I take brings me closer to my goals"

"I move my body with gratitude and joy"

"I am stronger than any challenge I face"

Let these words sink into your mind. Feel them become part of you, fueling your motivation and focus. Take one more deep breath in... and as you exhale, gently bring your awareness back to the present moment. Wiggle your fingers and toes, stretch if you'd like, and when you're ready, slowly open your eyes.

You are ready. You are capable. You are on this journey for yourself, and every step forward is a victory. Carry this motivation with you as you continue your fitness routine, knowing that you are building something strong and lasting.

CHAPTER TEN
TAKING CHAIR YOGA BEYOND THE CHAIR

Chair yoga is a wonderful foundation for movement, but as you grow stronger and more confident, you may find yourself wanting to explore beyond the chair. This chapter is about expanding your practice and finding ways to move more in daily life. You may worry about limitations, but know that progress is always possible no matter where you start. Here, you will discover how to safely transition into new movements, challenge yourself at your own pace and embrace a more active lifestyle while still honoring your body's needs.

TRANSITIONING TO MORE MOVEMENT

As you build strength and flexibility through chair yoga, you may start to feel more capable and eager to explore additional movement. This is inevitable. Don't be alarmed. Transitioning to more movement doesn't mean abandoning your chair yoga practice. You are simply going to expand on it. Small changes, like incorporating standing poses with the chair for support or increasing the range of motion in seated stretches, can make a big difference in how your body responds. But it is important as always, to listen to your body. Make your progress at a comfortable pace, and don't be in a hurry to take the next step.

Another way to expand your practice could be by adding gentle weight-bearing exercises to strengthen bones. You can also incorporate balance exercises to improve stability, or take short walks to complement your routine. If you have been practicing deep breathing and mindfulness in your chair yoga sessions, you can take those same principles into movement outside the chair. This will definitely make activities like walking, stretching or even daily chores more intentional and enjoyable. By gradually introducing new movements, you build confidence in your abilities without overwhelming yourself.

The beauty of movement is that it's adaptable to any stage of life. Some days, chair yoga might be all you need. And then you will have days when you may feel ready to stand, stretch, and move more freely. You just have to make an effort not to push yourself beyond your limits but to embrace the joy of movement in a way that feels natural and fulfilling. By gradually expanding your practice, you create a sustainable, long-term fitness journey.

EXPLORING DIFFERENT YOGA STYLES

Yoga is a vast and diverse practice. There are so many styles that cater to different needs and goals. As you progress in your chair yoga journey, you may find yourself curious about other styles of yoga that can complement your practice. Exploring these different yoga styles allows you to discover what feels best for your body, energy levels and lifestyle. Whether you want to focus on deeper stretching, gentle flows or relaxation techniques, there is a yoga practice that can support your needs while still being accessible and enjoyable.

For example, if you enjoy the slow, mindful movements of chair yoga, you might find restorative yoga or yin yoga particularly beneficial. These styles focus on deep stretching and relaxation, which can help with stress relief and flexibility. If you want something more dynamic, gentle Hatha yoga can introduce you to standing postures and breath-based movement while still keeping things slow and steady. For those who enjoy a meditative approach, Kundalini yoga incorporates breathwork and chanting, which offers a spiritual and energetic boost.

Let your body guide you as you search for what works best for you. Remember, you don't have to commit to just one style. You can even get creative with it. Many people mix different practices depending on how they feel each day. Some days, chair yoga alone might be perfect. Other times, you may enjoy including a short standing sequence or a guided relaxation session. This keeps things fun and interesting for you while still helping your body. Yoga is flexible and adaptable to your journey. So take your time, experiment, and embrace what makes you feel good, strong, and at ease.

GUIDED HATHA YOGA MEDITATION: A JOURNEY OF BALANCE AND RENEWAL

Find a quiet space where you can sit comfortably in your chair, with your feet planted firmly on the ground. Rest your hands gently on your lap, palms facing up. Close your eyes, take a deep breath, and let yourself arrive in this moment.

Take a deep inhale through your nose... and slowly exhale through your mouth. Feel the breath move through you, releasing any tension you may be holding. Let your shoulders soften, your jaw relax, and your mind quiet.

With each breath, allow yourself to settle deeper into your seat. Picture your body as a strong, grounded tree...your spine tall like the trunk, your roots extending from your feet into the earth below. Feel the steady support beneath you, holding you with ease.

Now, bring your awareness to your breath. Inhale deeply, expanding your belly and chest... then exhale slowly, drawing your navel gently inward. With each breath, imagine a warm, golden light flowing through you, filling you with energy and calmness.

With your next inhale, gently roll your shoulders up toward your ears... and as you exhale, let them glide back down. Inhale again, lifting your heart space slightly, and as you exhale, feel yourself relax deeper into this moment.

Now, shift your focus inward. Visualize a soft light glowing at the center of your being...your inner power. With each breath, let this light expand, radiating warmth and stability. This is your core, your strength, your balance.

Imagine that this inner light is aligning your body and mind, bringing harmony to every movement, every thought, and every emotion. As you sit in this stillness, remind yourself of your capabilities with the following affirmations;

"I am strong"

"I am present"

"I am enough"

Now, gently bring movement into your meditation. Inhale, and slowly extend your arms overhead, reaching toward the sky. Exhale as you lower them down with control, feeling a gentle stretch. Inhale again, and this time, twist slightly to one side, feeling a release in your spine. Exhale, returning to center. Repeat to the other side.

Each movement is an extension of your breath…slow, intentional, effortless. Flow between these gentle stretches, feeling the energy circulate through your body, awakening every cell.

Gradually return to stillness. Let your hands rest on your heart, feeling the gentle rhythm within you. Take a deep inhale… and a long, soothing exhale.

Before you open your eyes, take a moment to express gratitude…show gratitude to yourself…for showing up, for breathing….for moving with intention. Carry this sense of renewal with you throughout your day.

When you are ready, gently open your eyes…smile softly…and step back into the world with clarity, balance, and peace.

LONG-TERM WELLNESS GOALS

To create a lifestyle that naturally supports weight loss and overall well-being, you have to stop relying on short-term fixes. Sustainable health isn't about quick results. You have to focus on building habits that fit into your daily life and contribute to lasting change. Chair yoga is a great foundation. But true transformation happens when movement, nutrition, mindfulness and self-care all work together. You want to create a routine that feels enjoyable, not restrictive, so that staying active and making healthy choices become second nature rather than a constant effort.

One of the most important aspects of a long-term wellness journey as emphasized throughout this book is consistency. Small, daily actions add up over time. A 10-minute chair yoga session each day, a balanced approach to eating and staying hydrated are small and simple actions but they all contribute to steady progress. Beyond that, making conscious choices like prioritizing your sleep, managing stress and maintaining a positive mindset helps you to create an environment where your body can naturally shed excess weight and stay strong. The more these habits become part of your routine, the easier it is to maintain a lifestyle that supports your goals without feeling overwhelming.

Chair yoga and mindful living naturally evolves with you. As your body grows stronger, your energy improves and your confidence builds. You will naturally want to expand your practice and refine your habits. Whether it's increasing movement, exploring new healthy recipes or deepening your mindfulness practice. Each step moves you toward a more vibrant, fulfilling life. But as you grow and explore, always remember that long-term wellness is about making choices that help you feel your best, day after day, in a way that is both realistic and enjoyable.

CONCLUSION

As you reach the final pages of this book, remember that this is not the end of your journey. It is simply the beginning of another chapter in your lifelong journey toward better health, strength and well-being. Chair yoga has given you a foundation, a way to move, breathe and care for yourself in a way that supports your body and mind. Whether your goal is weight loss, improved mobility or simply feeling more energized each day, know that every step you take, no matter how small, is a victory.

There will be days when motivation feels low or life gets in the way, but consistency, self-compassion, and a willingness to adapt will keep you moving forward. Let yoga be more than just an exercise. Let it be a way of living. Think of it as a lifestyle that nurtures your body, calms your mind and uplifts your spirit. Don't forget to celebrate your progress! Embrace each challenge as an opportunity to grow and trust in your ability to create lasting change.

As you close this book, take with you the knowledge, confidence and inspiration to continue your practice. Your chair yoga journey evolves with you. Keep exploring, keep moving, and most importantly, keep showing up for yourself. You are stronger than you think and the best is yet to come.

YOUR EXCLUSIVE ACCESS

Thanks a million for being here. Your support means so much to me!

The best way to keep in touch with me is by signing up for my newsletter –
https://theawesomereaders.com/

Or scan the QR Code below

See you soon,

Aria Sage

www.ingramcontent.com/pod-product-compliance
Lightning Source LLC
Chambersburg PA
CBHW070538130626
46555CB00003B/1474